ISBN 978-1-332-82921-7
PIBN 10127687

1 MONTH OF
FREE
READING

at

www.ForgottenBooks.com

By purchasing this book you are eligible for one month membership to ForgottenBooks.com, giving you unlimited access to our entire collection of over 700,000 titles via our web site and mobile apps.

To claim your free month visit:

www.forgottenbooks.com/free127687

English
Français
Deutsche
Italiano
Español
Português

www.forgottenbooks.com

Mythology Photography **Fiction**
Fishing Christianity **Art** Cooking
Essays Buddhism Freemasonry
Medicine **Biology** Music **Ancient
Egypt** Evolution Carpentry Physics
Dance Geology **Mathematics** Fitness
Shakespeare **Folklore** Yoga Marketing
Confidence Immortality Biographies
Poetry **Psychology** Witchcraft
Electronics Chemistry History **Law**
Accounting **Philosophy** Anthropology
Alchemy Drama Quantum Mechanics
Atheism Sexual Health **Ancient History**
Entrepreneurship Languages Sport
Paleontology Needlework Islam
Metaphysics Investment Archaeology
Parenting Statistics Criminology
Motivational

314225

℃

California Society.

... PRIZE ESSAYS ...
—BY—
Scholars of the High School
—IN THE—
State of California,
UPON THE SUBJECT
"PATRICK HENRY."

The First Prize, a Silver Medal, was awarded to
PAUL G. CLARK
of the Los Angeles High School.

The Second Prize, a Bronze Medal, was awarded to
HOWARD D. EBEY
of the Los Angeles High School.

Honorable Mention, was awarded to
CHRISTOPHER G. RUESS
of the Los Angeles High School.

Committee on Award.
HARRY WOODVILLE LATHAM.

PUBLISHED BY THE SOCIETY
JUNE 17TH, 1895.

Sons of the Revolution

IN THE STATE OF CALIFORNIA

A PROCLAMATION.

To the High School Scholars of the State of California, Greeting:

The Society, Sons of the Revolution, was instituted on **Washington's Birthday**, 1876, in the State of New York, and it now has a **National Organization** modeled after the government of the **United States.**

The purposes of the Society are stated in our **Constitution:**

"**The California Society, Sons of the Revolution**, has been incorporated for the purposes of perpetuating among their descendants the memory of those brave men who periled their lives and fortunes in the War of the Revolution to wrest the American Colonies from British dominion; for the collection and preservation of manuscripts, records and documents relating to that contest for Independence; for the inspiration among its members and their children of the patriotic spirit of their forefathers; for the inculcation of a love of country and veneration for the principles which are t e foundation of our National Unity, and the promotion of social intercourse and cordial fellowship among its members."

Its membership is composed of direct descendants of **Ancestors** who, either as **Military, Naval or Marine** officers, soldiers, sailors or marines, or officials, in the service of any one of the thirteen original **Colonies or States,** or of the **National Government**, assisted in establishing **American Independence,** during the **War of the Revolution.**

The Societies in the Eastern States have erected monuments upon **Revolutionary Battlefields,** placed bronze and marble tablets at places made historic by heroic deeds, and erected a beautiful Bronze Statue in the City of New York to the memory of **Captain Nathan Hale,** ' the man who made the name of spy synonymous with martyr and patriot in the records of the **War for Independence."**

California contains no Revolutionary historic ground, but the **Sons of the Revolution** can erect a **Monument to Loyalty and Patriotism** in the hearts of her sons and daughters.

Now, Therefore, as an incentive to research in **American Patriotic History,** and to give them a more intimate knowledge of the patriotism, devotion, heroism and sacrifices of our **Forefathers, The California Society of Sons of the Revolution** offers them a **Silver Medal** as a first prize and a **Bronze Medal** as a second prize for the best Original Essays upon the subject,

PATRICK HENRY.

Competing Essays must contain not less than 1776 nor more than 1894 words, typewritten on one side only of paper 8x10 inches, with 1½ inch margin at the left, signed by a nom de-plume, accompanied with a sealed envelope with the nom-de-plume on the outside containing the writer's real name, address, school and a certificate from the Superintendent or Principal of the **High School** that the Essay is original.

All Essays must be sent by mail in a large or "legal" envelope to the **Secretary** of this Society before January 1, 1895. The examining committee will receive the Essays, the Secretary retaining the envelopes containing the real names of the writers, until the committee shall have reached a decision, when they will be opened at a meeting of the Board of Directors of the Society.

The prizes will be awarded at the annual meeting of the Society in **Los Angeles** on the anniversary of **Washington's Birthday,** 1895.

The Society hereby appoints the Superintendent, Principal and Teachers of each competing High School, a Committee of Review and Inspection, with authority to reject such Essays as may not be worthy of a place in the competition, so that only meritorious Essays be sent.

The Prize Medal is Silver, the face being a fac simile of the **Seal** of the Society, and will have, on the reverse, an appropriate inscription with the winner's name. The second prize will be like the first, but in Bronze. Both medals will be suspended by a silk ribbon in buff and blue, the **Continental** colors of the Society.

Given from the **Hall of our Society** in the City of **Los Angeles,** this eighth day of May, in the year of our **Lord** one thousand eight hundred and ninety-four, and of the **Independence of the United States of America** the one hundred and nineteenth, and of the **Society of Sons of the Revolution** the nineteenth.

[SEAL]

HOLDRIDGE OZRO COLLINS.
President.
ARTHUR BURNETT BENTON,
Secretary.
114 North Spring Street, Los Angeles, Cal.

STATE OF CALIFORNIA,
Department of Public Instruction,
SACRAMENTO, April 24, 1894.

HOLDRIDGE O. COLLINS, ESQ.,
President California Society Sons of the Revolution,
LOS ANGELES, CAL.

DEAR SIR:
The plan proposed by you for securing prize essays upon subjects relating to the War of the Revolution, meets my hearty approval. I commend it to the Principals and Directors of our High Schools, believing that it will prove a source of both pleasure and profit, and a powerful means of cultivating a proper patriotic spirit on the part of our young people. Very truly yours,
J. W. ANDERSON,
Superintendent Public Instruction.
[Copy of Proclamation.]

PROEM.

The California Society Sons of the Revolution was organized "for the purposes of perpetuating among their descendants the memory of those brave men who periled their lives and fortunes in the War of the Revolution to wrest the American colonies from British Dominion; for the collection and preservation of manuscripts, records and documents relating to that contest for Independence; for the inspiration among its members and their children of the patriotic spirit of their forefathers; for the inculcation of a love of country and veneration for the principles which are the foundation of our National Unity, and the promotion of social intercourse and cordial fellowship among its members."

Only those are eligible whose ancestors participated upon the Colonial side in the War of the Revolution.

The Societies in the Eastern States in carrying out the practical objects of the Organization have erected statues of distinguished men of the Continental Army, and placed bronze and marble tablets upon spots made memorable by heroic deeds.

In the early days of its existence the California Society determined, as an incentive to the patriotism of our growing youth, and the study of our most memorable epoch, to offer prizes to the scholars in the High Schools for the best two essays upon the subject PATRICK HENRY.

With the hearty endorsement and co-operation of J. W. Anderson, Superintendent of Public Instruction, Proclamations were sent to every High School in the State, inviting all scholars to compete for two prizes, one a silver and the other a bronze medal, to be the reward for the two best essays. A large number of responses was received and they were all referred for examination to Harry W. Lathan, A. B., a graduate of Yale College and a gentleman of discriminating literary ability.

The following was his report, viz:

" I return herewith, Essays Sons of the Revolution. I should advise the awarding of prizes as follows:

First Prize, Essay by Laru, No. 3.

Second Prize, Essay by Scribendum, No. 7.

Third Prize, Essay by Patrio T. Lover, No. 13.

H. W. LATHAM."

Upon opening the sealed envelopes containing these *noms-de-plume* it was found that " Laru " was Paul G. Clark, Scribendum was Howard D. Ebey, Patrio T. Lover was Christopher G. Ruess, all scholars of the Los Angeles High School. The medals will be given to the winners upon a suitable occasion, and this Society has the pleasure of presenting herewith the successful essays. The prizes are a fac-simile of the Seal on the first page of this pamphlet with an appropriate inscription on the back.

A similar competition upon another subject will be proposed at the next session of the High Schools of California.

The Silver Medal Prize Essay.

PATRICK HENRY.

BY PAUL G. CLARK.

Out of Chaos came forth order; out of blinding darkness proceeded a pure ray of light, out of the Revolution Patrick Henry, like Athena, was born.

It seems as though often in the crisis of a nation's life, whether for the first time the Ship of State is being launched upon the sea of national life or whether it approaches too closely upon some mid-ocean shoal, that in the moment of its direst need, some deliverer arises in his saving might. Perchance the nation is about to fall a prey to a voracious enemy or be the blameless object of a tyrant's oppression; maybe, discord prevails in the breasts of her sons and the state about to succumb to the intestine rivalries of dissension. Such at one time was the seeming fate of America.

Voyagers had set out from the land of England and planted a colony upon the virgin continent of America. Its ranks had been recruited from time to time, until at last it no longer depended on the land of its nativity for support. It took firm hold in the soil of its adoption and spread its roots over a large extent of country. A stately stock shot up from the center of the plant; in turn upon it grew a branch, then another, until upon the majestic stem of popular unity there stood, in the grand beauty of peerless nature, thirteen branches.

This country has ever quickly rallied around the standard of freedom whenever assailed by seditious spirits. The king of Britain raised his hand and dangled the chain of servitude before the eyes of North America. The people saw the pending danger about to force them into abject servitude. America arose in her new found might and delivered her one ultimatum, "Give me liberty or give me death!" The fiat had gone forth; there is no appeal from the exalted judgment of liberty.

Who is this who has raised such a burst of patriotism from the people without a government? Who has had the courage to throw down the gauntlet of defiance before a nation, lord of priceless possessions? Who has raised the standard of Independency over. a country crushed by its master's heel? Let the patriotism of America answer. Those who feel the priceless value of liberty give a continual and ever-living response. Upon the heart of every true son in this broad land are engraven these mighty words—Patrick Henry.

Patrick Henry was born in Virginia in the lap of liberty, and cradled in her arms. The true date of his birth was when America declared her freedom.

The first years of his life were spent outwardly in idleness; yet all the while that he was doing nothing for his own advancement, neglecting education, making failures in commercial embarkations, he was amassing to himself powers of observation, comprehensions of his fellow beings and such secret keys to the human character as were of lasting benefit to him throughout his life. Literally he absorbed experience from the silence of the woods and learning from behind the plow. Nature was his schoolmistress and man his educator.

But slowly and surely fate was working out his destiny. Already were signs of an wakening in that mighty intellect; already was the power of his genius stirring like a giant awakened from sleep, until he is found bursting over his hearers the bombshell of his eloquence; driving his opponents from their seats in the violence of his invective; transfixing them with his brilliancy. Such was the beginning of his public career.

The whole of his talents was devoted to his country's service; all of his life devoted to it upon the rostrum of independence. Long, manfully and faithfully did he battle with the enemies of his country; first, in the House of Burgesses before the war; afterwards in the Virginia House of Delegates; then in the Continental Congress; and finally (not abandoning his country when, largely through him, her independence was declared) in the Constitutional Convention, where with all the innate powers of his mind opposed what he, in defiance of the choicest intellects of the country, thought to be America's foes; where he battled with all the powers of his vast intellect, and finally, through his influence, procured a series of amendments which are the present balances and safeguards of the Constitution.

Retiring from the arduous duties of political life, Patrick Henry had more laurels to win at his profession, the bar. At last, however, wishing rest from a public and more or less political life, he sought the retirement of his home. Even here he was pursued, and the turmoil of politics penetrated to his door. The People of Virginia could not forget one of their foremost representatives and truest patriots. The Legislature of the State offered him for the third time the chair of Chief Executive of the Commonwealth. In the midst of his family, most cherished friends and intimate acquaintances, a public career had no further charms for him. His service to the free and independent States of America had been rendered; he possessed the consciousness of having done his work, and owed not a single duty to his native State. Let others take it up and support what he had helped to create.

Once more does the sea of politics wash its breaking waves around the quiet of his home. Upon his ear falls the whisper of possible civil dissension; and this old man, well worthy to rest in peace upon his laurels and to live upon the patrimony of his estate, leaves the restful quiet and solitude of his home, and seeks again to support the State which was his creation. It was his last effort, and when there sounded in his ears the call from heights above, it found him at his post, denouncing tyranny, exalting liberty.

If ever a passion animated the breast of Henry, it was the love of Liberty. Filling his whole soul, it permeated every nerve and fibre of his being. It prompted him to deliver his heaven-born message of eloquence. Whether in the assemblages of the Continental Congress, in the House of Burgesses, or in some small gathering, he never failed to impart to them the lofty enthusiasm of his soul. Never did his oratory fail in its forceful effect. Always rang the resonant cry of his voice for liberty, filling his hearers with admiration only exceeded by their patriotism. Before them played the lightning of thrilling words, and rolled the thunder of patriotic persuasion. When we think of Henry, it is as the grand patriot-orator; those high flights of genius which were inimitable; those soul-stirring exhortations which in their potent effects produced a silence like the depths of the sky.

Even before the idea of a national independence had fully forced itself upon the people, it was foreseen and understood by Patrick Henry that that was the thing which the future had in store. Accordingly it was his lofty spirit which sounded the first clarion note of "to arms." 'Twas he who voiced the opinion of America and proclaimed it in its ruling body. Like magic the colonists saw what he had long foreseen. His burning words were having their effect. The torch of independence was lighted by his own steady hand. He roused the enthusiasm of a people almost stunned by the shock of oppression. The chains of restrained liberty were cast off and the country rose, a nation. True, oh Patrick Henry, that Cæsar had his Brutus, that Charles 1st had his Cromwell, but it may be said with equal truth that the chief Powers of Civic Thraldom had their Henry.

The record of his life shows the prevailing qualities of moderation in both speech and action. The love of justice amply made amends for whatever he lacked in the routine of his profession.

Nero's power would have been crushed before he could touch his imperial sceptre had Henry lived in his time. The historians voice would have been dumb concerning the tyranny of the Pharaohs had Henry existed before the Christain Era. No soul could listen to his "silver tongue" and remain impassive. Patrick Henry roused it on to action and quickly cut the Cord of Fate for America's deliverance. He was the Rienzi of American history.

His was the magnificent grandeur of the lion. Calm and peaceful when un-aroused, yet grand of contemplation; but when once disturbed from his tranquility, he rises in majesty and plunges with the roar of a mighty thunder into the thickest of the fray. On he rushes with the force of the ocean wave before which all smaller objects are crushed as the twig beneath the paw of the forest King. Anon he pauses; yet only to gather force for one mighty effort; when beneath a master stroke of superb power, the arguments of his opposers lay crushed at his feet.

Let destruction sweep from shore to shore, let devastation blow its lurid breath across the three thousand miles and more, or discord cast its fearful shadow across the land; let war wrap the American bulwarks in darkening smoke and the capitol dome crash because of Anarchist's deadly power, yet above it all will shine the bright star of American patriotism, the star of the man who told England to stop her tyrannical rule: the star of the man who made us a nation, whose bright star of destiny will guide us to the future as it has lighted the past. The glorious fate of our land is inevitable, the rising sun of her glorious future as yet is only flashing its golden rays in the ether of the East; her eagle of progress but commenced to wing his flight across the years of her existence; the waving Stripes and inspiring Stars only started to head the march of the long, winding column of Freedom's sons; still from the mighty company there rings the cry of their "hail to the chief," for it was the author of the Resolutions against the Stamp Act, who with a few straggling followers began the now endless march.

It is to him that there peals from the soul of Americans the thrilling music of patriot strains caught by the rolling orbs of time to hand the secret on to eternity. It is the message of gratitude from Columbia's sons and daughters, and though the earth and heaven should roll away, from the bottomless depth of space will spring the fount of a people's thanks. Its twelve streams of crystal drops of love will sparkle forever across the boundless waste of time, spanned by the rainbow arch of deserved reward.

Patrick Henry! A name to be extant when heroes are no more; when the names of kings are buried beneath the grandeur of their glory. A name to sound along the "corridors of time" and echo through the labyrinth halls of fame. America can never forget the cornerstone of her independence, her champion for the only priceless jewels which are the sole heritage of her sons; she can never forget the true advocate of her Freedom, the Protector of her Liberty. LARU.

The Bronze Medal Prize Essay.

PATRICK HENRY, PATRIOT AND ORATOR.

BY HOWARD D. EBEY.

Almost two hundred years have been born from the tragic stage of time since a lustrous star, obscured by the haze of humbleness, joined the constellation of American greatness. When oblivion's claim to Washington's immortal name is granted by a grateful people, when America no longer loves the light of liberty, then only will its splendor wane. May 29, 1736, conscripted from the realms of pre-existence by the angel of destiny, Patrick Henry donned the mantle of mortality and went forth to fight for freedom.

Home was the most beneficial schoolhouse for him, and the lad's lack of education excelled his love of study, just as he communed more with God's wild woods than with the weak words of man. As he grew older, taught by dame experience that fate had fashioned him neither for the country counter nor the poor plantation, he elected law as his vocation. A steed of fleetest foot it proved to be, and bore him by the shortest road to fame.

His native county was the field of his first trophy. The clergy had been paid with the Virginia's depreciated currency and worthless weed. They demanded indemnity. The "Parson's Cause!" The people's counsel forsook them; the clergy's hopes sprang up like hydra's heads; the cause had Patrick Henry's hand and heart. A Hercules, he wielded well the severing sword of popular prejudice, and seared the wounds with blazing eloquence. The verdict petrified the vanquished with amazement: "One penny damages."

Time rolls on. The House of Burgesses beholds him. The Stamp Act is law. Words are well-nigh worthless weapons now. A lull of suspense pervades the land. Loyalty or liberty! That is the question. Age and experience hesitate to decide; youth and inexperience determine to act. Patrick Henry becomes the leader of the legislature, the orator of Virginia, the statesman of America, as he pens the "Virginia Resolutions," declares America as free as

England, pronounces the principle that "taxation without representation is tyranny," as like a seer, he says, "Caesar had his Brutus; Charles the First his Cromwell; and George the Third ["Treason!" cries the chair. "Treason!" echoes the house. Silence reigns and the orator maintains his course]—and George the Third may profit by their example. If this be treason, make the most of it." Thus was the flag of freedom unfurled. He rang the bell of liberty; though fear attempted to muffle it, its peals rang in the colonists' ears, nor has its sound yet ceased.

The years glide by, and his practice in the higher courts lessens, as he forgets himself in remembering his country. In the First Continental Congress, he strikes the key-note of union and success with the words: "All distinctions are thrown down. All America is thrown into one mass. I am not a Virginian, but an American." He is in Virginia's Second Revolutionary Convention. The sound of war is on the wind, and it inspires him. His voice is the voice of God as he says, "The war is inevitable. And let it come." His hearers' souls are thrilled as he utters the words, "I know not what course others may take, but as for me, give me liberty, or give me death."

The royal governor planned to sieze all munitions of war. Powder was transferred from the public arsenal to an English man-of-war. Virginia's sons arose in arms, eager and prepared to fight. But caution, fearful, called out, "Disperse, ye rebels," and they dispersed. Hearing of this, the people's hero, Patrick Henry, at the head of several undaunted hundreds marched on to Williamsburg. Success! His majesty's receiver-general makes amends to the amount of £330. Not a gun fired, not a man dead,— Virginia's bloodless Battle of Lexington was a victory! "A certain Patrick Henry" was denounced by the governor's proclamation, but the people praised and loved him.

The hero's talents were recognized, and during the recess of the Second Continental Congress he represented Virginia.

Commander-in-Chief of Virginia's soldiery! That was the commission, but it was *only* a commission. He renounced his title, and another chapter of his history was written.

The question of independence agitates the minds of Virginia's statesmen; Patrick Henry's counsel: Let us have a declaration of independence, but let us *also* have union at home, and friendship abroad. It is embodied in the resolutions. In the constitution of Virginia, he sows the seeds of democracy and equality; in her declaration of rights, he asserts for the first time the divine principle of religious liberty.

Just one day after the adoption of the Declaration of Independence, the patriot becomes Virginia's first governor. During this term an illness befalls him which determines his future. As governor, he devotes his time and talent to the common cause in the darkest days of the Revolution. His second administration is remembered for his thorough loyalty to Washington in the cabal to supplant that general with Gates. While he was governor a third eventful year, the fair and fertile fields of the South were ploughed with the cannon-ball and watered with the blood of heroes. In these three years, Virginia thrice invested her able and patriotic governor with exceptional authority.

He refused to succeed himself for a third time by a loose construction of the constitution; he declined to serve as delegate to the general congress. Nor did the duties of statesmanship at any subsequent time call him beyond Virginia's borders.

Virginian villages saw the unsheathed sword. From place to place the capitol kept moving. And once it came to pass, that, told in time that Tarleton the Terrible was not far distant, the luckless legislators fled on horse and foot for safety. And many and most comic are the tales told thereof,—of Patrick in particular.

During four years Virginia watched her ex-governor in the legislature with pleasure. After Cornwallis' surrender, strong in his convictions, obedient to the dictates of his conscience, he advocated with magnanimity and Demosthenic eloquence the return of the British refugees and the freedom of trade—even with discomfited England. He essayed the solution of the Indian problem, and sought to make all men religious. And now, honored once more by his people, he occupied the governor's chair for two terms.

A few years more passed away, and in the projected surrender to Spain for five and twenty years of the Mississippi, America's artery, the South's discerning statesmen see the serpent of sectionalism. Would the North barter the South's rights away! Never! Patrick Henry, from being Federalism's firm friend, becomes her foremost foe, and refuses to attend the Constitutional Revision Convention, and thus tacitly submit.

The Constitutional Convention adjourns Sept. 17, 1787; June 2, 1788, Virginia's Convention convenes with her orators, patriots, and statesmen there—but divided. Ratify the document unamended? " Yes," says statesman James Madison. " No," says statesman Patrick Henry. Why Patrick Henry's " No?" A strong central government,— but *also* the rights of the states expressed and not implied— this he advocates. But his own words answer—" I mean not to breathe the spirit nor utter the language of secession. The first thing I have at heart is American liberty; the second is American union.'

Defeated! He had expected it. One fourth of all the words had been struck from the mint of his mind and, grateful for the respectful attention shown, he magnanimously vowed the vow of patriotism—he would correct the constitution constitutionally.

When Virginia's assembly met, was Patrick Henry vanquished? No. Washington wrote to Madison, "He has only to say, 'Let this be law,' and it is law." He named the senators, carved out the congressional districts, and by untiring labor secured the consummation of his grand object, for, on December 15th, 1791, the constitution had ten amendments.

Now, as a lawyer, he set one more gem in the diadem of his fame. Could a British subject collect a debt, due before the revolution, and paid, according to law, into the loan-office of Virginia? Counsel for the defendant, Patrick Herry answered that question negatively. The past and the present, law and learning, his own mind and the minds of others,—all these he laid under tribute, and when, the legislative halls deserted, he came forth to argue the British debt cause, he was victor before the battle.

As an advocate, he knew naught but success. Humor, passion, sympathy, love, patriotism, reason, and religion— he appealed to them all. He entranced the ear, caught the eye, touched the heart, moulded the mind, and—conquered!

And now, lawyer, soldier, statesman, orator, and above all, patriot, he retires from the arena of public life. The amendments made, he is a warm friend of the Government. In 1794, Governor Henry Lee appoints him senator; President Washington in 1795 offers him the portfolio of state, and, the next year, the chief-justiceship; in 1796, he is chosen Governor for the sixth time. White with the snows of age, bowed down with infirmity, he must decline these honors, one and all. But his country needs one more "transient effort.' Madison's "Virginia Resolutions!" Jefferson's "Kentuky Resolutions!" War with France! Partisanship rampant! Archibald Blair, John Adams, George Washington—cry out to him. The appeal is heard, and in the hour of his country's peril he is a candidate for the assembly. The orator's prophetic voice is as a voice from the dead. He is elected—but never again does he cross the threshold of the assembly, for he has made the peroration of his life.

He goes home and soon breathes a last prayer for him-self, his home, and his country. Good and faithful ser-vant of God and man! Thy spirit is fled—thou art gone. When Washington joins him in paradise, the double loss is felt and America's eyes are wet with the tears of sorrow.

His happy home, with his children playing around him, could be likened only to heaven. His law fees had been mod-erate, and prudence alone had enabled him to provide for his large and beloved family. The company and conversa-tion of his friends gladdened his heart; the sweet reveries of solitude delighted his soul. Generous to his friends; he displayed magnanimity toward his foes.

His habits were exemplary; his life was a book of moral precepts. The fragrant weed of his native state never enslaved him; he waged war against intemperance in a practical manner by introducing a light beverage. He deplored the blight of slavery while he felt its necessity, knew its convenience in his day.

Talents, success, fame, never clothed him with vanity. His life was profoundly religious; his belief was mirrored in word, deed, and example. Human throughout, he breathed with humanity. Conscience was his only master; perfection his only idol.

Never did he hesitate to lift his voice for liberty; a lover of democracy, a destroyer of tyranny, he was a maker of history. In the book of fame, Clio penned his biography in characters of gold; today patriotism punctuates it with the diamonds of his eloquence. At birth, genius made her abode in him, with strains of ecstasy; in life, midst patriots' lays of adoration, victory's eagle perched upon his stand-ard; at death, leaving a vacant chair in liberty's house, he was greeted with the angels' songs of welcome.

PATRIO T. LOVER.

Sons of the Revolution.

IN THE

STATE OF CALIFORNIA.

OFFICERS FOR 1895.

President
HOLDRIDGE OZRO COLLINS,
> Los Angeles.

Vice-President.
MAJOR WILLIAM ANTHONY ELDERKIN, U. S. A.
> Los Angeles.

Secretary.
ARTHUR BURNETT BENTON,
> 114 N. Spring St., Los Angeles.

Treasurer.
JOHNSTONE JONES,
> Los Angeles.

Registrar.
EDWARD THOMAS HARDEN,
> 2331 Thompson St., Los Angeles.

Historian.
JAMES MONROE ALLEN,
> San Francisco.

Chaplain.
REV. JOHN GRAY,
> Rector St. Paul's Parish, Los Angeles.

Marshal.
FRANK CLARKE PRESCOTT,
> Redlands.

CPSIA information can be obtained
at www.ICGtesting.com
Printed in the USA
BVHW041049170119
538075BV00017B/1141/P